LANGUAGE BE MY BRONCO

A Life in Poems

Jim Brown

Psychosynthesis Press
LANGUAGE BE MY BRONCO
A Life in Poems

© 2012 by Jim Brown

All rights reserved. No part of this book may be reproduced in any manner whatsoever without written permission of the author except in the case of brief quotations embodied in critical articles and reviews.

Psychosynthesis Press
P.O. Box 1301, Mt Shasta CA 96067
ISBN 978-0-9611444-9-4

Cover photo by Alexander Lowry ©1962
"Rio Grande River from Otowi Bridge, New Mexico"
(Used with permission)

·

Technical Editor Ted Slawski
Set in Adobe™ Garamond Premiere Pro

The author and publisher gratefully acknowledge the following publication in which two of these poems first appeared: *Moving Mountain* ("Rose's Kitchen," "Summer Solstice, 2006"). "The Whole Year Round" was previously published in *Held in Love*, eds. M. Y. Brown and C. W. Treadway, Psychosynthesis Press, 2009.

Dedication and Acknowledgements

I dedicate this book to Molly Brown. Had it not been for Molly's heartfelt urging, and her generous offer to publish it through Psychosynthesis Press, the book would not exist.

Along with Molly, a few long-time friends stretching back twenty years or more have encouraged my inborn motivation to write—and especially to write poems. These include Susan S. Scott (an accomplished poet), Francine Foltz (a champion of poetry education), Tim Burns, Gary Foltz, and Caroline Rackley (who have offered gentle and wise critiques). I extend my appreciation to these friends for keeping the current flowing long enough for me to get to Mt. Shasta, where some powerful tributaries brought the current to its present magnitude.

I'm referring to the fine poets I have met and befriended since moving to far-northern California about nine years ago. My heart swells with gratitude as I remember how I have benefited from their steady moral support and coaching, how much I learned simply by being in their presence and hearing them read their work over the years.

Foremost among this sterling group is Michael McMahon, whose dedication to bringing high-quality poetry to this tiny town, and to enabling local poets to share their work publicly, catalyzed my entry into the poetry open mic experience. Of the distinguished poets who participated in the Writers Series program that Michael initiated and coordinated for several years, I feel particularly close to Charles Goodrich, Clemens Starck, Jerry Martien, David Lee, and Paul Hunter.

All of these people had a vital role in swelling the stream of poems that flowed out of me in the past few years, the period when most of the poems appearing in this book were written.

Finally, I am grateful to the local poets with whom I served on the advisory board of the Mt. Shasta Writers Series, and with whom I often shared the stage for open mic evenings—Jill Gardner, Maria Fernandez, Charlie Unkefer, Michael Zanger, and Carly Furry—not only for their friendship, but also for setting such high standards of writing and thereby spurring me to attend constantly to the quality of my own work.

Introductory Remarks

Since I choose to represent the written pieces in this little book as poems, it occurs to me I had better say a bit about what I think a poem is, and what distinguishes poems from other kinds of creative writing.

As I see it, most poems present images of a moment, or a series of moments, which lit up the poet's soul and caused a memorable shift in understanding. Building on such moments, the poem then goes further, creating a connection between the moment and a larger context out in the world. Through this connection, meaning comes into existence. The whole point of writing it down is to let other people in on it, offer others the opportunity to experience or reinforce a similar shift in understanding.

Creative prose can do the same thing ultimately, but typically features abundant description of characters and setting, interwoven with plots and subplots, on the long way to building connections. What makes a poem distinct from a prose piece (leaving aside such issues as meter, rhythm, rhyme, and line structure) is, I think, the economy with which the writer sketches the moment and teases out the connection between the moment and the context. Ideally, the connection comes across, if it is sufficiently pithy and pregnant and elegant, as a verbal ZAP! It has a strong emotional component, which may or may not be followed by mental insight. Either way, a shift happens, and relatively quickly.

I think of Japanese haiku as the most exemplary form for economy of expression: the imagery is minimal, and the link to a larger world is merely a whisper in the mind's ear.

I have tried my hand at *haiku*, but found it too confining, too rigid for my western lack of disciplined restraint. What you will see in this book are pieces that straddle my respect for economy of expression and my love of ebullient flow. The spirit of haiku often looks over my shoulder, but just as often the shades of Kerouac, Cassady and Ginsburg tug at my arm saying, "c'mon man, let's go!"

Come to think of it, those two forces—*haiku* and beat— in various forms account for much of how my life has unfolded. Which brings me to the rationale underlying the subtitle. As it happens, these poems do directly reflect essential aspects of my life—and, I'm betting (as all poets do), the lives of many who read them.

Jim Brown
October 28, 2012

Contents

I. "We shall not cease from exploration…"

    Working With The Deep Blue 2
    Don Juan's Table 3
    Half Asleep With a Glass of Wine 5
    Formations 6
    Snow Maid 8
    Serial Dreaming 9
    Noticing the Genesis of Wanting 14
    Traversing the San Rafael Swell, Central Utah 16
    Teaching Dream 19
    Variation on a Dream 20
    Reflections on Midnight Snow 21

II. "Severe truth is expressed with some bitterness."

    Blast 24
    A Call to Wildness 25
    Post-industrial Pony 26
    Anticipating Thanksgiving 27
    New Year's Eve On a Really Big Ship 28
    ain't no blues like the texas existential blues 30
    Note to Mankind: Don't Bother Bob 31
    Along the Edge 32

III. "And Now For Something Completely Different!"

    Language Be My Bronco 34
    Ditchdog 35
    Wu Li Pendulum Moves 36
    I Wonder 37
    Niçoise 38
    For Us To Lure 39
    Fighting Form 40

Mickle Knights of Old   41
He Had Been Carefree All His Life   42
Following My Finger   43
Spring   44
I've Been a Hog Farmer   45
Slow Talker   46

IV. "I'm so glad, I'm so glad, I'm glad, I'm glad, I'm glad"

For Susan, Who Encourages This   50
Molly Laughs   51
Rose's Kitchen   52
Dawn Maiden   53
Journey by Night   55
The Grave   56
Re-Thinking Kerouac   57
A Lot of Life is Occupied   58
Early September Saturday After the Grateful Dead Hour   59
You Are Invited…   60
January 15 – Night Snow Followed By Sun   61
The Trail   63
Berkeley Brown Shingle House   64
Summer Solstice 2006   65

V. "The clouds that gather round the setting sun…"

Roots To The Sky   68
Sour Harvest   69
Short Days   70
Cool Wind   71
Notes on Everlasting Memory   72
Slow to Reach Out   73
To Enter the Clearing, Or Not   75
Elegy In Falling Leaves   76

VI. "Celebrate, celebrate, dance to the music..."

    For Ben, Who's Eight Years Old   80
    Now   81
    For Judy, at 60   83
    Harmonic Re-Convergence   85
    For Greg-at-41   87
    Grateful Dead   89
    Cass, 39   90
    The Snow Beneath Cassiopeia   92

VII. "...the happy highways where I went and cannot come again."

    Adolescent Nights   96
    Growing up on the Pajarito Plateau   97
    Memories of the Mesa   98
    With Us Now   99
    Raven Etiquette   100
    Someplace I Belong   101
    A Morning in the Sun   102
    Cathedral at Sand Flat   103
    June 17, Rain   105
    Seven Scandinavian Women   106

VIII. "When we have shuffled off this mortal coil"

    The Northshore Trail   110
    Kinder Options, Please   111
    Wings   112

I

"We shall not cease from exploration..."

—T. S. Eliot

Working With The Deep Blue

One wakeful night while
working with the deep blue, I said
to myself:

You are a whirling, pulsating
precipitate of the evernow.
When you encounter others like yourself,
together you might concoct irrelevant structures
and pay them too much mind,
and begin believing these structures are important
in defining you all and
dictating your functions.

Big mistake (I went on to myself). Too complicated.

Yes, I said, hook up with the other precipitates—
all you can.
Then—do what is easiest:
whirl and pulsate with them.

Something might come of that;
it's nothing you need to make up.

⌒ Don Juan's Table

I dream about sitting at don Juan's table
beneath the portal of his small house
in Sonora.

In the near distance, stark mountains
loom beneath storm clouds.
We are eating

tortillas and beans spiced
with tiny hot peppers.

The shaman sits to my left, chewing
peacefully. I have been thinking,
don Juan,

of what you said about the vast
possibilities when no one
is at home.

He savors his food, watching me—
Yaqui-style—without turning his head.

I continue: It seems that if
there is no one at home there is no one who
can suffer harm.

He nods, his eyes flickering with humor
as lightning flickers over the mountains.

Even, I ask,
from drugs or alcohol?

                That is so,
he replies (flashing a smile like the sunlight
that breaks through the gathering clouds),
if there is truly no one at home.

Now
thunder rumbles from deep within him
or deep within the mountains—I cannot tell.

Half Asleep With a Glass of Wine

Half asleep with a glass of wine
in one hand and Marquez's latest novel in the other,
I opened my eyes to set them down
only to discover I held no glass, no book.

The place on my shirt
where I had washed out a stain was still damp.
Images had fluttered in my brain as I
reached the edge of sleep,

as if my senses still reached out
to grasp the situation. But it was
of the past, not of now, that they told me.
Time had folded up like a poppy,

leaving impressions to emerge
free of tyrannical reality, free
to reorder themselves according to hidden schemes.
Madness. Dreams. I thought I had better write it down.

Signal headquarters.

Formations

Of the ancient people now called Anasazi,
in a band that occupied the favored
southern portion of the vast
table land we now call Mesa Verde,

there was, I imagine, a hunter who
followed a faint path (that he himself had worn)
over the rim and down through
a watershed, along a creek that he knew
attracted turkeys, deer, and elk,

where he would lean invisibly against a tall pine tree
in the mild sunlight of early spring and wait
for movement signifying game, an encroaching enemy,
or the subtle wavering of air displaced
by spirits whose presence he often felt.

Following that trail so often he would, naturally,
note and remember unusual rock formations
that reminded him of dreams or visions
around the fire at night,

and that formation would take on
meaning as a marker of his descent
into the verdant hunting ground
below the rim.

Formations like that
line my own path over the rim,
reassuring me that my descent to wait
and watch for what may come my way
in the cool shade of verdant forest

is real, has purpose, is more
than the shimmering stuff of dreams
or campfire visions, even though
that is what the formations
bring to mind.

Snow Maid

Through a diamond glass I glimpse
a figure kneeling, leaning back and to the right,
features snowy white and softened
slightly by the night wind. Her arms, curved,
hold only space against her icy breasts.

All through the afternoon as she took shape
the daylight faltered. Flat and gray,
it washed away the figure's features.

It takes the moon-abetted mystery of night
and facets of a beveled window-pane
to bring the snow maid fully into sight.

Serial Dreaming

In pre-dawn mountain chill
I turn in my bed, waiting
for the sun to be awake.

A sudden breeze outside
shakes a shower of dark leaves
toward the autumn earth, each

ridden by a dream. One by one
the dreams detach
and drift into my restless sleep.

4:07 a.m.
Spurred by deep craving to roam freely
over the land, I follow a dim path
through a defile, skirting gray stones
shaped like wolves. Words—
I cannot make them out—are scratched
into the rock.

The defile opens onto
a perfectly square plain. Hooded figures
line the path, which lays
a maze-like course within the square.
The hooded ones murmur
to me as I brush past, offering me boundaries,
and safety within them.

I listen and agree to stay, accepting the safety
and restraining my wandering.

Still, every step I take in the maze brings
sharp longing for what is beyond.

4:12 a.m.
A dozen students sit zazen in a grassy enclosure,
arranged in a semi-circle. Our teacher claps her hands,
once, and begins leading us in *katas* based
on animal movements. One student improvises
on the Kneeling Zebra, adding a a back-kick, left
then right. Another tacks an unconventional
forward roll onto the Rhinoceros Trot. Our teacher
joins in, bringing her impeccable style
to these antics, then captivates us by transforming
the Striking Cobra into a shimmering Mongoose Leap—
making the two appear simultaneous. Many of us
run to put on costumes, snatching up beads,
jerkins, scarves, quickly fashioning masks out of
bark and leaves and lily pads.
Ecstatic, we dance in a circle.

4:25 a.m.
Part of my mustache comes out by the roots, and I begin
shaving off the rest of it while listening to Fred Allen
on the radio. Grandad wanders in to listen with me. Soon
we are chuckling together over a story Allen tells
about a Spanish spring. The story ends abruptly.
I promise Grandad I will find out what a Spanish spring is.

4:30 a.m.
A family of superbeings, many
of them young, display their abilities in a formal
chorus. The central couple, Moon Man
and Moon Woman, enact a soap opera episode:
he asks her to marry him
and bear his child; she at first refuses
because somehow this would curtail
her own super-activities. An image
superimposes on this scene of
a freeway (a superhighway?)

with a wide turnout.

4:38 a.m.
I am about to take a written exam
to be administered by a Sufi, Robert Ornstein.
Listening to his instructions, I
hear an undertone of "don't take this shit
too seriously." I try to remain suitably light,
yet some anxiety creeps in. Distracted
by uneasiness, I pluck from his beard two
whiskers that are noticeably longer
than the others, then realize they must have
religious significance.

Before beginning the exam I find a seat
that will enable me to get help
from another student, a young woman who
arouses me sexually.

(At this point
the dream begins to fade. The final image
is of a wide-mouthed jar.)

Half awake, I imagine writing Ornstein a note
in lieu of the exam saying
"I accept an F in the course, but
having made love to a wide-mouthed girl,
take an A in social relationships."

I lie still enough not to dislodge the dream memories
until I bring them to the recall stage, then reach
for my water glass and notebook, noticing
it is not yet 5 o'clock. I scribble the main images, settle
back into the warmth of bed, listen to the breeze
still sighing, the trees still creaking. Breathing
slows down. Muscles slowly release...

4:56 a.m.
Warily, I skulk through a town empty, apparently,
of people, trying to escape the notice
of a gigantic tiger. At times I glimpse him
bounding along a parallel street, always
just a block away. He is hunting
        for me.

The streets are snowpacked, with berms for me
to duck behind when I sight him. In this way I manage
to avoid detection, after which I try to put more distance
between us. But always when I see him he is just
a block away, huge shaggy head swinging back and forth,
those terrible jaws open,
leaping incredible distances.

Certain I am almost out of time, I stumble into a muddy lot
littered with old cars and car parts. In its center, a large shack,
leans against the weak sunlight. A ramshackle overhead door
is open, and I dart through it to uncertain refuge. Inside, two
diminutive men in greasy coveralls and caps, faces begrimed,
surrounded by the detritus of a backyard auto shop,
watch me calmly.

Unable to speak, I gesture desperately toward
the street, where the tiger has appeared and caught my scent.
As he gathers to bound toward the shop, the two grease monkeys,
moving as one, heave an engine block toward the beast.
Growing even more huge, he pounces on it and mauls the steel
as though it were meat. They glance at each other; one hoists
a radiator and slings it at the tiger. They watch as the monster

shrinks slightly and attacks the radiator. The second mechanic
tosses a generator just inside the door; the tiger
leaps at it, shrinking even more. Next comes a distributor,
then a water pump, then a fuel filter,

followed by a PCV valve, each savagely
attacked by the rapidly diminishing cat. A spark plug
brings him down to kitten size, and they sweep him into a tool box

and close the lid.

5:10 a.m.
I awake, breathing rapidly, and wait
for the last dream to release me.
Outside, pale light reveals trees swaying,
leaves falling.

The spring-fed waters of Castle Lake, on the fringe of the Castle Crags formation opposite Mount Shasta, are famously pure and clear. While wandering one day along the lake's northern shore I noticed the tell-tale ripples of fish feeding close-by, and began to sight trout swimming in the shallows. As I watched these torpedo shapes dart beneath the water's surface, my gaze suddenly focused on a slow slithering motion right on the lake bottom a few feet from shore. It took me a couple of seconds to realize I was seeing a water snake on the hunt.

Never before in my long life had I seen anything of snakes in water but their heads above the surface as they swam at the apex of a snake-sized wake. Never had I imagined they could stay submerged for very long, yet now I saw one stay beneath the lake's surface for ten minutes or more. During that time I moved slowly along the shore studying the snake's meandering progress, how it paused near submerged branches for camouflage. It literally vanished except when in motion.

ᘓ Noticing the Genesis of Wanting

Sitting on a cold, flat rock,
so close to the upper Sacramento
I can dip my hand into its frigid water,
I lean back against a smoothly rounded boulder
that perfectly fits my lumbar curve.

Upstream, the Eddies, draped
in dark conifers laced with snow,
sit perfectly still under arching blue sky.
Striate clouds emerge and fade,
emerge and fade as the sun edges
behind a stand of tall Douglas fir
forty yards south of the winter-shrunk river.

Rocks, water, sky,
sun, trees and mountains shimmer
upside down on glassy surface

of pool formed by low, curving
wall of rocks carefully placed
to mute the river's rush to a soothing gurgle.

Kin to the pool without ripples,
without purpose or want I sit
still as the mountains,
still as the rocks around me,
immersed in the easy movement
of sun   trees   clouds.

                                            Long moments cradle the stillness.

Then something in me names it: peace.
Peace, the cessation of wanting.
And just past the instant of naming
comes an instant of wanting more
of this, more peace, wanting it to last—
comes a ripple in the stillness.

      I watch
as peace gives way and wanting emerges,
hushed and subtle as a serpent.

I do not miss the peace, feeling instead
a thrill of discovery, a familiar sharp pleasure
that always accompanies
an unexpected sighting
of a natural event.

I notice also
that the interlude of sheer peace
has tempered my wanting; I am content
with one new sighting today.

Traversing the San Rafael Swell, Central Utah

1.
Been across it in all seasons,
but mostly in the summer. Once,
the long steep grade and brutal sun
overwhelmed the cooling system
of my little Honda CRX,
black as my grandfather's dominoes,
forced stop at scenic overlook
to cool and contemplate the vast
dry pans and peaks, the flat blue sky.

Peaceful, except for the constant blatting
of I-70 truck traffic.

Easy to hallucinate
a strung-out endless flock of monstrous metal sheep
bleating and farting across this bleak, broken land—
a land useless overall but
grand and hazed with mystery.

Easy to imagine the desert fathers
who claimed it for their sanctuary—
thick-bearded patriarchs, their eyes fierce and cunning,
their heads clogged with prophecy, their bones brittle with pride,
their lustful loins unchained to populate
this arid, empty, ancient land.

2.
In the snow-mantled uplands of Northern California,
that waking dream comes back, revives
an image of desert patriarchs

moving tribes and flocks
over parched land sprinkled

with enough watered groves to sustain them,
but not enough to share with others.

The men firmly grip their staffs,
eyes slitted against the harsh sun,
to guard against marauding wolves and lions
and competing Semite tribes.

Chewing stems of psychoactive desert plants
and grasping after any meaning
to justify this meager life,
they postulate a higher order of existence;
argue and contend their longing
into a deity.

Where would such a god abide?
In this desiccated, tumbled,
alkali- and salt-pervaded place they prowl
with their flocks and clans to seek
uncertain sustenance? They look around,
ponder, and conclude: "Not here…
not where we spend our blighted lives.

"No, He has to be up there, somewhere in the sky.
Some place other than this earth from which
we scratch a skimpy living.
Separate from us, higher, better view."

Once launched on such a bitter thesis
the next step has to be:
"We must look like schmucks to Him…
goddam!
Goddam schmucks—look where we live!
Got to be something we can do to raise
our estimation in the eyes
of this abstraction we have flung

into the skies..."

Thus these desert patriarchs
cursed themselves and us
with imperfection, judgment,
the cruel codes that judgment spawns,
the endless machinations we concoct
to lift ourselves above our self-
inflicted imperfection—
and the rampant, needless misery
these curses pile upon
the daily struggle to survive.

3.

The dream unravels to its end.
I dwell in mountains, not the desert,
and do my best to deconstruct
a heritage so ill-conceived and parched.

If our roots were flavored forest green
instead of saltbush and desert bramble,
and our branches unfurled in verdant glades
instead of twisting in to guard
scant molecules of brackish water,
we might feel freer to embrace the earth,
ourselves, each other, everything alive.

Teaching Dream

In a dream I undergo
mystic teaching and initiation in the secrets
of modern magic; they involve
creation via words.
For a time within the dream
I comprehend many subtle techniques—
ways of shading reality, ways of augmenting it.

Awake now, still I know
that dreamy comprehension lives in me
within some mutable membrane
floating in a moving pool, and that
when it leaks through the membrane it will change the pool.
It will change everything.

Variation on a Dream

The cat-woman stood limned
by the window
in the half-light of dawn.
Between us,
a tossed quilt, still warm.
My mind, caught
in the half-light between languor and
shock, arced with the question:
Have I
been here before?

Downstairs,
when the light was stronger, I closed the door
and, still not knowing, glanced up
at the window.
But by then she had gone.

Reflections on Midnight Snow

After midnight I lay down my book and rise
to switch off the reading lamp, sleepy
and ready for bed. Glancing out the window I see,
dimly lit by the streetlight a hundred feet away,
steadily falling, mesmerizing snow;
it slants across the streetlight's glow,
driven by a stiff wind from the south.

I stand at the darkened window watching this late winter surge,
drifting into a trance, imagining the snowfall on the mountain
on this stormy night, how much harder it must be falling,
how much stronger the wind, and how up there—
say at the rocky overlook I often visit above Sand Flat—no light,
no light at all, shines to show it falling,
nor is there any warm-blooded above-ground animal to look up
to see it
even if there were a light.

With theta waves taking over my brain there is barely
time enough to wonder, as Schrödinger might have,
whether up there the snow really is driving
hard, invisible and unknown, or if that
is a scenario waiting to exist only when an observer
shows up. If so, would my imagination
be observer enough?

Would I then be cosmically culpable as I fall asleep
and the image fades away to nothing?
Will the akashic police be waiting
to bust me, when I wake up, for obliterating reality?

I wonder if Shambala can assign me a good public defender
...or
maybe...I can find a wormhole to a parallel universe

with more lenient views,

more tolerance

for a careless...sleepy...destroyer

of deep...dark   swirling

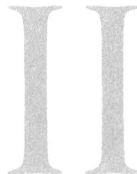

"Severe truth is expressed with some bitterness."

—Henry David Thoreau

Blast

Born at the end of the Great Depression
and quickly maimed by industry
and inattention,
I have lurched through life
a mood-bomb, sentient enough
to be stunned by my own slow
explosion.

Pausing by a plaza in the grip
of jittery adolescents—
their lips and lobes pierced,
their eyes snaking with desire and confusion—
I watch as they try to connect
but manage only to score.

Chilled by insight I glimpse,
shivering, the shattered mirror
whose fragments
reflect this scene in countless
variations. The waning days
of Western Civilization
have cast

a mood worthy of my muted rage.
Strangely at home among
these pathetic
life-forms, I loosen
my casing and consider
the possibility of having
a blast.

A Call to Wildness

Wildness I admire has uppermost just two features:
getting with the lightning force of creative juice
and disregarding the social impediments
to that force.

Wild women and wild men let it rip
with some combo of these two.

Let us empower
the wildness in each other.

Post-industrial Pony

I raise my sympathetic glass
to you, the gadget-ridden.

The fatty that forks your saddle, alas,
keeps on gaining weight.

For so long you were simply
"rode hard and put up wet,"

as my cowboy ancestors
used to say;

that is not your current problem,
poor horsie.

All along, you whinnied
your approval of

the swelling giant that
presently bends your back, and now

its tumid bulk repays you
by riding you into the ground.

Anticipating Thanksgiving

The fifth rainy night in a row
following a long string of golden days—
snow above 4000 feet—
and the stone faces of Mount Shasta
may be buried deep under the cover
laid down by this protracted storm.

The light in my living room
no brighter than needed to read and write by;
fire ticking in the stove; poems by Snyder
and Starck in easy reach. Add jazz on NPR,
a splash of brandy to honor the rain,
and the latest polling results on the eve of
a monumental election, and this prayer spills forth:
May our strengths and virtues soon return
from their long and tortured exile, from the drought
that has drained our souls.

New Year's Eve On a Really Big Ship
12/31/08
titanic: having great magnitude, force, or power
—*Webster's New Collegiate Dictionary*

Under way for scores of years, gaining bulk and momentum as it goes, the vessel
known as Industrial Growth Society has steadily disabled its navigation systems
and plowed, stupid and proud, into waters that are suddenly deadly. A vortex
vaster by far than the oversized ship
has appeared just ahead, and the officers on watch squint and scratch their chins
and argue about whether to reverse engines and change course or ignore the damn thing because
to veer off would disturb the rich folks at their parties.

A new skipper is due on the bridge soon. Passengers are mostly glad about that and revving up new celebrations, although some are on deck looking at the vortex and wondering if the new skipper can mobilize what's needed to keep the good ship IGS
from being sucked down and torn apart, or—
and this is the 64 trillion dollar question—
whether that is even possible any more, given the mass and momentum of this monstrous craft; wondering too if they could get lifeboats into the water
or just jump overboard,
and whether even that would keep them from the vortex (how close is it?
they cannot tell). As they mill around, maneuvering for optimum access to the lifeboats, they jostle and threaten each other.

The topside orchestra eases into the soothing strains of
"Auld Lang Syne;"
drinks and smokes appear, bearing the implicit invitation to look away,
look at anything but the vortex, relax a bit and celebrate,
despite what they know is ahead.

The moment bulges with strangeness.

ain't no blues like the texas existential blues
(an anthem for the occupiers)

fight brewing in a bar in amarillo
little guy says to the big guy
wait right here
goes to the juke box
drops money in
picks a blues song
comes back starts moving to the music
big guy throws a punch
little guy slips it dancing

outside a flock of starlings
creates an inky pattern swirling
against a cloudy sky

inside the big guy throws punches
little guy dances and ducks

question for y'all

does the big guy stop punching
and start dancing

or does he just slump over
exhausted

either way the starlings
they got nothin' to do with it

Note to Mankind: Don't Bother Bob

Bob gave you everything:
puffed your poor life into its wobbling orbit
(leased the orbit, arranged the payments).

What prompts you to strut like a peacock as
the orbit begins to decay beyond redemption,
then break into a blind
stumbling run, mindless
of the wall between you and
the wrecking yard? You seem so surprised

when you slam into the wall.
Stunned and bloody, you fumble
for explanations unworthy
even of your faulty dream memories.

When those fail to explain the wall
and the blood, you look
to Bob; don't bother.
Bob gave you senses

and sense; use them.
Stop strutting, attend to your orbit.
Believe in the wrecking yard, and above all lift
your head and appreciate
the wall.

Along the Edge

I could be at home
in a sweet little house perched
near the edge of a bluff
rising straight out of the Pacific Ocean,

listening night and day to the waves
hammer the rocks below, beat against the bluff.

Turning my head I would see
other sweet little houses perched
along the edge,
their owners outside listening to the waves.

Our days are numbered; the great ocean,
the relentless Pacific, will claim us all.
We pour our wine, raise our glasses,
salute each other.

III

"And Now For Something Completely Different!"

—Monty Python

Language Be My Bronco

Language be my bronco;
swift me bumpalong over rock and rill
challenges of folded ground, unfenced ranges.
Drink deep from streams fresh with meaning,
my cayuse!

Syntax my saddle be,
cinched tight so no slipping
as gallop through sage
thought thickets;
nuance, my reins.

I will sleep safe in
your circling moon-shadow
while you graze on sweetgrass
word fodder, and silent mustangs
surge through my dreams—

until, dawnbathing, we join
yet again, horse'n'rider,
to lope beneath the listening sky.

Ditchdog

on his morning prowl,
cuts a random path
between a broken curb
and a gritty brick wall;
questing   questing—
bam! goes still as a stone,
bellies down tight, nose twitching,
twitching,
while a serpentine breeze ruffles
his thick neck hair.

Paleomammalian brain spins
limbic loopty-loops around
traces of a scent—the only whiff
capable of driving away
all other canine considerations—
a bit salty, musky,
redolent of—
y e s!
Ditchbitch!

She was here; her delightful effluvium
lingers still.
She is close enough to find, and
find her he will.

Wu Li Pendulum Moves
(Please forgive me, Gary Zukav and Itzhak Bentov)

If you understand how a Möbius band
enfolds that third dimension,
and action at a distance
doesn't tax your comprehension,

and if you grok how adjacent clocks
seek to tick in synchrony,
just accept the force that sets our course
when you vibrate next to me.

If you long to pat Herr Schrödinger's cat
and collapse its q-wave function,
then you will not fear to join me, dear,
in virtual conjunction

and anoint your belly with quantum jelly
while we embrace in hyperspace
and belt our chorus in the cosmic torus
so the gods know we're amongst 'em!

I Wonder

what it would be like to join
the army, own a railroad,
run a whorehouse, drive a semi;

cure an illness, write a
classic, plant an orchard;

start a range war,

blow a kidney, win
the lotto, run on empty;

quell a riot, please
the ruler or do
the Continental.

I wonder
if satisfaction is possible by
keeping kosher, cleaning rifles,

switching parties, acting crazy, riding
western, pleading guilty, starting over,
digging deeper, playing possum,

speaking plainly, growing quiet or
granting mercy.

Niçoise

If I could find a woman
sporting the taste of a Niçoise olive—
oh that woman, that woman, oh
how she would suit me!

A taste fully realized
yet not over the top.
A taste that stays strong
bite after bite.

Winds of mystery
blow through Provence
while my mind stamps its feet
on the Riviera sand

and my bared teeth tear
at the mistral winds, seeking
the source—the precise vector—
of the Niçoise olive taste.

For Us To Lure

For us to lure the Faerie Folk
we must achieve their mischief.
Take you then my outstretched hand;
twirl within my arm toward me
'til your breath comes hot upon my cheek
and hot upon your breast, my palm.

With such a stance we might attract
the elves, the sprites, the nymphs and leprechauns;
and if they balk I know we could devise
an escalating dance they won't be able
to withstand.

Fighting Form

Wherever he went he sensed there were eyes
studying his movements, looking for a clue
to his fighting form.

So when he walked he walked stolidly,
belying the fluid turbulence his body
could assume when provoked;

and when he danced he pumped his arms
vertically, with a hint of jerkiness,
concealing the low unin-

terrupted flow that could swirl out
a lethal stream of possibilities.
Did this strategy

of disguise serve him well?
On the question of its
combat value he did not dwell.

He knew only this: although untested,
the practice kept him
fresh and interested.

Mickle Knights of Old

Leather, tough as iron and studded with bronze,
creaks, and weaves the forest light—
alerting the larch, the oak and the yew:
Knights of Majyk are on the move. I hasten
to beseech them:

O merciful and mickle Knights of Old,
grant me leave to try my hand
at latent skills, confidently raising
female juices, craftily evading
the attention of gruff guardians.

May each day bring fresh opportunity
for leaping, illicit joy—mutual
yeses binding two into one,
building to oneness on and on

forever, 'til— *clang!*   There it is,
the Voice of Responsibility—
and it's back to earth for ye, laddie.

O mickle Knights, I do not seek
to silence altogether
that stringent Voice, but only, with your help,
      to fashion a delay

between the yeses and that Voice, a space
within which mad Shakespearean frolic
      may take place.

He had been carefree all his life
in a worried sort of way;
then he won the superlotto,
and there was hell to pay.

He had it made beyond his dreams,
but he had learned enough
about the terms of chaos to
suspect it would turn rough.

All that wealth to manage—damn,
he longed to do it right,
to put that lucre to good use
so he could sleep at night.

He had kith and kin across the west
he wanted to help out,
and causes upon causes
toward which to point the spout;

a means to get from here to there
that wouldn't dirty up the air;
land to grow organic veg
(natural capital to serve as hedge

against the crash he knew was coming);
and time to spend on healthy strumming
along the sensual parade
before his senses thinned to fade.

Being poor had plagued his youth,
and now that he had gold
he would have more work than ever
to do as he grew old.

Following My Finger

When I paused to think, I thought:
it's funny how I—
I was following that finger.
Astonishing, really—
it was my finger,

it was always my finger
I was following.

Like, "'alf a mo',
that was my finger
I was following."

A part of myself, you see,
connected, ultimately, to
every other part of myself, to
every other part of reality;

I was following
all of that, I was
following all of that.

∽ Spring

A *welling up*
or *coiled bouncing*
like bears in a Disney flick.
Not the bears around here, no:
Spring comes, they just wake up
HUNGRY! Stay out of their way, Jack.
They got to feed themselves and
those little'uns who appeared
magically in the dark cave
while the snow swirled
outside, found the
teats, drained
their mama down
'til hunger woke her up.
Come Spring, everything
wakes up hungry. Buds hunger
to burst from branches; bugs swarm
in hungry bunches; earth hungers
for the sun's warmth. Two
hunger to become one,
and one to become
a multitude.
It's life, see, and
life hungers to go on.
You will know this when
you awake to Spring and your
genuine appetite for life takes over.

I've Been a Hog Farmer

I've been a hog farmer and I've been a hog
(my essence arcs over the glistening fog).
The woods and the heathers, the copses and caves,
they court me, beguile me, while shrinking away.

Though lava-born boulders may go on forever
(forever surrounded by granular stars),
the edge of my essence cavorts without scheming,
spins unforeseen patterns like spume from a wave…

like spume from a wave when sunlight slants through it
and fans out in colors that tumble and shift
into patterns the singular I might intuit
before the chance winds can scatter the spray,

the edge of my essence might fleetingly stay—
persist long enough in the glistening fog
for me to imagine myself a hog farmer,
and also imagine being a hog.

Slow Talker

Among the several things I know:
I read too fast and talk
too   slow.

Gulp poetry, blaze past the nuance—
but speaking brain just wants
to slowdance.

The words are queued up 'round the block
and shuffle forward when
I talk.

But as each one gets past my face,
a hundred
stack up
in its place.

On the enneagram I'm stuck
in fifth position, damn the luck!

I'm busy stashing information,
and can't be bothered with oration.

The Broca region of
my brain
is stuffed so full it gives me pain.

Still, all of that could change,
I feel;
I might deliver quite a spiel—

forego the joy that all fives prize,
put down the books
and vocalize.

Might even spend a month
 or three
in dialogue and colloquy;

release the choke-hold
on my tongue, and spill my words to dance among

the euphonetic paragraphs of those who elocute
for laughs.

"I'm so glad, I'm so glad, I'm glad, I'm glad, I'm glad"

—Cream

∽ For Susan, Who Encourages This

In mid-step, crossing
the street, I am
graced
as a lens pops into existence
and glides
through my senses.
Suddenly lucid my brain
registers the light, the air.

They dance, I am lifted. glimpsing
as I first did
decades ago
the mysteries-in-waiting.

Are they everywhere?
Or is it just the light, the air?

Molly Laughs

After writing down the creek sounds
Molly laughs—three descending notes
that now merge with the gurgles
of the creek and tumble with them
to the Pacific.

Molly laughs in the ocean.

Rose's Kitchen

Jake the Rake stopped by Rose's house
to inquire about the gunshot
he had heard early that morning,
found her in the kitchen, naked (except for her boots)

and spattered with blood, a butcher knife
in her fist, a deer's hind quarter
on a plastic tarp on the floor,
her eyes wild. She waved the knife at him.

Don't just stand there gawking, she spat,
go get the rest of it out of the canyon!

Back-tracking the blood trail
he had no difficulty finding the carcass,
rolling it into another tarp, slinging it
over a broad shoulder. Scrambling out
of the canyon he smiled to himself,
remembering her sanguinated

sixty year old body, Barbarella-trim,
leaning over a hunk
of half-skinned venison
on the kitchen floor.

࿇ Dawn Maiden

Dawn maiden edges forward
delicately exposing
    the eastern horizon.
Stippling the sky
    with modest pinks and blues, she waits,
    advances, waits again,
        then surges
    unrestrained, brazen.

Buxom morning takes command,
    her power mounting
    with surprising speed.
She tumbles hours together
    recklessly, like rocks in a mountain river,
    until they spill out into afternoon--
        losing momentum,
    worn smoother.

Past meridian
    the hours settle into the softer
    more yielding bosom of a matron.
Events march in
    a cadence honed
    by deliberation
and the premonition
    of loss.

Bread, broken
and consumed, embodies
    the memory of morning light
    and eases the transition toward

Darkness. The dowager simply appears—

        with no permission and
        little fanfare. Under her sway
The straightforward dramas of the day
          give way to subtlety and circumspection;
          how else could a consort as spare as Orion
              remain such a prominent partner?

They dance, Orion and the matriarch,
          their steps perfected by eons of practice,
          so stately as to escape comment.
No one can say with certainty
          when the earth/sky dance approaches
          nullity, that inevitable moment
              of disengagement
        when

Midnight mother slips away
          over the hills, sighing a familiar tale
          involving a serpent and a rodent.
A long pause, silence
between drum beats;
          Orion, appearing indifferent
        to the separation,
            glides toward
                  the horizon.

Abruptly, at an instant
              appreciable only by them, birds
              break the silence, excited
              to be the first to notice as

Dawn maiden edges forward . . .

Journey by Night

After turning off the light
I pause by my open window.
Warm night smells
charge my nostrils;
my pulse quickens.
Instantly I am ball lightning
streaking over that moonlit mountain,
careening off that lone cloud,
'til I scatter like elf-dust
over the hayfields and vineyards beyond.

I reckon there is enough of me
to leave some there;
gather up the rest
and put it to bed.

The Grave

It was truly happ'n'n' at The Grave
on North Rio Grande Boulevard,
Albuquerque, late spring, 1958,

a basement bistro, just enough light
to play chess, drink expresso,
listen to the Brubeck Quartet.

One Friday night word got around—
after-hours party at The Grave—
beer the beverage, bongos the sound.

In a mellow groove, fellowship unfolding,
wrapped in rhythm, I surrendered,
left the world of time and holding,
gathered cushions, and fell seamlessly asleep.

I don't know how, but in that blacked-out
basement chamber the light of dawn seeped
inside my eyelids, pulled me gently
from a dream and woke me,
rested, alert, serene, content.

The feeling bubbled up that there was
no one I had to answer to, nothing
to answer for—no why and no because.

Free as I have ever felt, I gazed
at other scattered sleepers, brothers all,
stood up and quietly exited The Grave.

Re-Thinking Kerouac

I could be getting out of the car in Needles
at this time of day and year,
checking into a Super 8 motel,
and I would still be awed by summer twilight lifting
the stucco walls of houses on this edge of town
to their highest color, bouncing
off the semis on I-40, and bringing
a glow even to the dingy west-facing drapes of
room 206 (non-smoking, cable tv, wireless access).

Instead, I am taking in the mid-summer sunset
from the front porch of my Mt. Shasta home.
Nothing fancy this evening: blue
blending into pewter, some wispy pink clouds,
the trees pristine in polarized light;

and I am flooded with joy
to be Off the Road.

A Lot of Life is Occupied

A lot of life is occupied
with pretending to remember
what just happened, convincing
whomever we think we have to convince
that we're with it, that whatever they're promoting
is as important to us as they want us to believe it is.

Lately, though, an alternative world-view has been
nudging my attention. It is this: happiness
consists of swaying, sashaying and
twirling in just the right
proportion.

Early September Saturday After the Grateful Dead Hour

I seem to be getting more than I should
from this—it feels a little trite
to spin around in wonder, head back,
looking at the stars (there's Mars)
and welcoming the wholeness,
believing the part of me that is meat may be the best part
and has certainly served me honorably.

When I stop spinning, my ears catch up
to the crickets rocking out in a pulsating chorus
reminiscent of the music I enjoyed earlier—sounds
that bring to mind this thought:
wave dynamics.

Escuchen conmigo amigos,
y hablen cuando quieran.
but remember what is around the talk:
wave dynamics,
weaving all around and through it.

With the Dead as with the crickets, beats
eventually emerge to entrain the mad
idiosyncratic fiddling of every single member
of the band. Synchrony rhythmically
augments amplitude and there it is: the cricket pulse.

The meat part of me catches the beat;
pulses pace my body's spin;
and when I look back at the skies
the galaxy has joined right in.

꧁ You Are Invited…

Come sit with me a while.
With silence and with words we will create
a place for your power, a magnetic center.
Moments will slide toward us and
break open,
spilling bright tendrils of possibility.

Let one take your inner gaze;
it may illumine your path. Let another
twine 'round your feelings;
it may draw you into the vast pain
all of us share
or it may tumble you into
joyful connection beyond imagining.

Many will simply usher you
again and again to sit calmly with your power
as it deepens.

We cannot know in advance
which tendrils might spill forth.
We can and will hone our attention—
they will not scatter unnoticed.

January 15 – Night Snow Followed By Sun

The cul-de-sac in front of my house:
usually a quarter-acre of ugly gray pavement,
now a graceful sweep of glistening white;
slant of morning sun
glances off its pebbly texture;
only when sun climbs overhead
will snow appear satin smooth.

A few tire tracks meander the circle
revealing neighbors' cappuccino excursions
and idiosyncratic driving patterns
(who hugs the curb? who splits the middle?).

No one stirring on the street; no footprints
mix in with the tire tracks—houses sit
blank-windowed, orderly and silent
until the first shoveler shows, followed
by the first blower.

                Next,
from the house directly across,
emerges Spokesman for Ascended Masters,
with his non-ergonomic shovel
wielded like a short hoe in itinerant Salinas lettuce field.
His lanky frame stoops to the job, gets 'er done.

I will wait, thank you, for the sun
to melt the four inches of new powder
off the south-facing slope of my driveway.

A quarter-mile beyond Spokesman's house
a dignified stand of Douglas fir;
beyond that, a mile or so
the shadowed cleft of canyon

where the Sacramento tumbles
down from birthing springs and cataracts;
above that, sweeping slopes of evergreen folds
grizzled now with clinging snow;
and over it all, the crisp jagged edge
where the Blue of the Sky begins—
unbroken blue! Bright and endless—
the like of which I have not seen
since late November.

Clouds will roll in later; time right now
to boot up for outside hosannas.

The Trail

It draws me on—
the trail.

My legs, no longer leaden,
thrust me forward.
Unsupervised, my feet
find square centimeters of firm grip.

Shoulders loose, head
balanced and light,
body gliding cleanly, registering
only a whisper of a jolt
with each step.

Around me scintillant molecules
of hilly air, like genuinely smiling hosts,
usher spring sounds, wood sounds
to my receptive ears.

My nostrils, questing
fox-like,
bring me organic news.
Undulating heat currents brush
past my skin.

On graceful slopes ahead and above
groves of live oak randomly fling
shafts of sunlight into my eyes while
cloud shadows slide across distant meadows.

Within this pagan temple
I waft, born by my senses.
No time, no duty; only this trail
and a partly melted self.

Berkeley Brown Shingle House

The scene haunts me as archetypes do:
hefty wooden furniture, earth-toned, dark,
in the parlor of a Berkeley brown shingle house
half hidden by mature trees—
live oak, bay laurel, Monterey pine—
on a shady street, quiet in early morning fog
that pushes through the Golden Gate
and tumbles over coastal ridges,
        carrying the tang of marine air

from a vast ocean-of-a-future, a sea
cosmically pregnant with abundant unknowns.

Summer Solstice 2006

The whole year 'round, from my front porch
(except for days-on-end of snow clouds, rain clouds)
I watch the sun set behind every bump and dip
of the mountain skyline, from north of Mt. Eddy
to south of Castle Crags.

Tonight, a few hours before summer solstice,
I stand just outside my front door and note once more
the sun's intersection with the skyline, hidden
behind the slender trunk of our neighbor's cherry tree.

The door and the tree establish themselves
as cardinal points of observation
for this annual event.

After I am gone, my successor
might continue the observance, and so on
until the cherry tree, the house, are gone.

Long after the age of human observers
the Eddies and the Crags will shift and crumble
and be gone, but the planet will continue
tipping one way, then another, as it circles
the sun, the ancient one that subsumes
all we are and all we know.

The earth, the sun, in far off temporal frames
we cannot imagine,

will themselves be gone.

But what of this joy?

"The clouds that gather round the setting sun…"

—William Wordsworth

Roots To The Sky

Once towering among other
red fir giants here near Panther Meadow,
moss dripping down its trunk like chartreuse paint,
this tree toppled to the south, overcome
by the north wind of a long-ago winter.

With its roots to the sky it lies lopped
into rounds the size of Volkswagens.

A crater twenty feet across once held
these roots. Now a chaotic tangle
sprawls next to the gaping hole, a mass
of serpentine tendrils crusted with an amalgam
of dry dirt and boulders torn from the earth.

I picture myself here to lend an ear,
to the red fir as it fell, to create
with my hearing a sound to mark
its demise; try to imagine—
would it have been a groan,
a scream,
or a stoic, shuddering
crash?

Sour Harvest

Pick a bunch of grapes in early spring
and crush them—no wine will come from that.

Most of my good right hand was crushed in early spring
in West Texas, when dustbowl winds howled,
when my childhood was just beginning.

Seven decades later, while spring winds lift
the chemical-laden soil of West Texas for its
annual distribution to god-knows-where,

my body, now safe in Northern California
where spring winds spread only snow-squalls,
still recalls the harsh season and unforgiving land

that hosted its accidental mutilation
at such a tender age—the crushing
of most of its good right hand.

Celtic tribes widely celebrated spring
as the season of bursting forth, when life
pushes aside obstacles, asserts its primacy.

For me, spring still ushers in a muted
aura of disaster, and the deep regret
of wine that never will be tasted.

Short Days

The days have grown too short, and
I do not cherish winter.
A mangled hand and crushed veins—
I can hold one ski pole real good,
the one on the left.

Gravity and velocity dictate, however,
that my right hand hold one too;
two to remain safely upright.
Haven't found a glove that keeps that one warm enough.
Winter brings a certain pain.

Global warming sounds
secretly good to me. Oh, I know
about coastal cities and villages
being inundated by polar ice-melt,
about planet-wide eco-havoc, all of that.

And I know I could theoretically move
nearer the equator;
but dammit I like it in Mt. Shasta.

Except when the days grow too short.

Cool Wind
(For Diane Gilman)

May these days uncoil
without fear.
Each one
has its special hue,
worthy of profound attention—
such as children bestow
on events that commonly slip
beneath the notice of their elders.

When rain whispers
over the water,
embraced by cool wind,
will your heart
welcome the wind and move
with its power
like a sail?

Every coil surrounds
a center that appears
      empty,
except to a billowing heart.

Such a one finds,
as the last loop plays out,
not emptiness but room
to run before the wind.

Notes on Everlasting Memory

From my current level of age-enhanced experience,
I can tell you confidently:
it takes more than the piquancy of a nipple,
the curve of a hip, or the lurk of a Venus mound
to set a woman into your everlasting memory.

To illustrate this assertion, a thought experiment:
I walk into a ranch-style in, let's say,
Sweetwater, Texas. An older neighborhood—sidewalks
swollen and broken by elm tree roots.

I find her in the living room sitting primly on the edge
of a loveseat from Furniture World,
her ageless image a little blurred. Her second husband
(the first died, I think, of a coronary), grayer
and paunchier than I, stands at her side.

An old acquaintance, I explain.
His eyes sharpen; hers remain unfocussed.
He speaks: What do you hope for, coming here?
That you would ask that, I say, so that I could let it be.

I turn my head toward her. Do you have anything to say,
Burnell? I gaze at her, bothered by what I cannot see.
Of course no answer comes, and that, too bothers me.

I leave the two of them in the twilight house, knowing
that I will probably return, driven
not by a torrid history,
but by its interruption.

Slow to Reach Out

Soon after I had learned to walk and,
walking where I shouldn't, fed
my curious right hand to moving gears
that turned a drum that mixed up dough for bread,

two fingers disappeared right off that hand,
and simple, carefree learning-as-I-go
vanished at that instant from my life,
replaced by tactics others see as slow.

The trauma forced me to a cautious, halting,
watchful mode in which I stretch my mind
as far into the future as I can,
probing every angle I can find

before I make a move—especially
one involving reaching out
with hands or heart—it doesn't matter;
either can be, have been, cut.

This tactic has some benefit for me:
my mind has gotten flexible and quick—
in itself a source of pleasure—and
liberated from the thick,

viscous heft of body and the
turbid sloshing of emotions,
has flown above the forces that
can disrupt its heavier companions.

The downside of the tactic, which I
hinted at before, is that while
I check the scene for safety I
might overlook a secret smile,

neglect a nod, or fail to act
upon the unplanned, softened glance
and involuntary leaning forward
that indicate a readiness to dance.

If I could pacify the lifelong
fear still buried in my brain,
born in a flash of somatic terror
and reaching instantly to entrain

my mind as guardian to make sure
that hand would suffer no more shock,
it could release my mind from ancient
servitude, it could unblock

the narrow application of
its scouting power, and release
that power to apply to ventures
that bring more love and joy and peace.

To Enter the Clearing, Or Not

How many times have I died, I wonder,
walking straight into the clearing
unwary of cudgel, shaft or claws?

How many lifetimes have I squandered
lurking around the clearing's fringe,
searching endlessly for traps?

The ancient tension haunts me always.
Every day of this life
I yearn for a middle way.

⁂ Elegy In Falling Leaves

Janis, I wish you could have been there today
with Molly and me on the oak-wooded slopes
below Castle Lake. I found a perch on a low, smooth
stump, cushioned around the edge with lichen,
as comfortable as any raja's campstool.

Over my right shoulder I could glimpse
Mt. Shasta's white flanks gleaming
through Douglas fir and oak branches.
Late afternoon sunlight slanted in from my left,
backlighting amber and yellow leaves of oaks, tall
and slender and still. My heart slowed with the peace
of a brilliant day, the *Dia de los Muertos*,
and my blood swelled with the colors.
I thought of you

as I have often in these past weeks
since I read about your death, but today
without the stabbing pain of loss and regret.
Instead of grief, I felt a tender longing
to share with you these moments bathed in beauty.

If you had been there you would have recalled
with me the moments you and I have cherished
amid brilliant gold and red aspen groves
above tall-grass New Mexico mountain meadows
half a lifetime ago—the sharp,
full-hearted love we shared.

But you were not there...
and as I watched leaves releasing
their tree-grip and fluttering to earth
I felt a pang of closure, a swirl
of sad relief. I can at last release

the hope that you and I might find
a way to reconnect as seasoned friends,
the fantasy that has haunted me
for decades.

Your absence from my life is now
beyond recourse; now I can begin releasing
the grip on that greener part of my life, dissolving
the fretful bond of memory and hope.
Now I can let the fantasy of reconnection fall
to the composting earth,

just as those leaves I watched today
fell slowly, one by one,
to join their fallen predecessors—
until suddenly a cloud of leaves
responding to a wayward breeze
tumbled madly down around me.

Janis, you rascal—was that you?

"Celebrate, celebrate, dance to the music..."

—Three Dog Night

For Ben, Who's Eight Years Old

You may remember seeing in your dreams
an arc of colors floating in a mist
that rises from a waterfall and seems
to touch your cheek, as though you're being kissed.

The arc is light, sent here by the sun,
that shines like magic through the mist and spreads
out into seven colors—red is one
(and seemingly the softest of all reds)—

then come orange, yellow, green and blue;
then indigo and violet appear
along the arc's lower edge where you
can barely see them.   Also, can you hear,

within your dream, the gentle whisper sound
that leaves make when they flutter in the breeze,
and smell the fragrance rising from the ground,
and feel the mighty presence of the trees?

I hope your life will always bring the joy
of hearing, smelling, seeing, feeling all
the wonders nature gives while you're a boy.
 I hope your dreams stay strong as you grow tall.

Now *(For Jen and Greg)*

Can you recall the time before,
knowing you were waiting to begin
your lives;
making a consummate skill
of waiting;

each knowing the pungent forest
with only half your heart and it was good
even then,
yet the breeze playing
over the horizon, tantalizing,
raised a yearning
spilling into pain—remember?

No need to wait longer;
let pain spill into joy. Yearn only
for spirit to embrace you both.
Walk together at dusk
to the emerald pools; let your
hearts reflect in unison
the thrumming of canyon tree frogs.

No need now to wait;
walk together at first light
to the farthest reaches you can imagine,
to the peaks beyond Kathmandu.
Bathe your feet in snowmelt
and your hearts
in each other's warmth.

Give full attention now to the dawn
of your emerging. Let its light play
among your deepest shadows,
not to dispel them, no—

to seed their creative power.

Walk together in the fullness of the day
to places of beauty that will appear
as you walk, sharing your unique knowing
of that beauty
and your unique dreams of beauty
when you rest from walking.

Wait no longer; join now
in continuous beginning.

For Judy, at 60

Chief teller at the bloodbank, who
can play the vein game through and through
(has done more sticks than most),

she'll soon declare that she is free,
say phooey to phlebotomy
and move on down the coast.

Nurse Judy swoons for ancient stuff.
Old furniture? Can't get enough,
nor quell the urge to strip it.

She'd like to have more figurines.
Been known to look through magazines
in search of the odd snippet,

the offbeat fact. She has to find
fresh fodder for her questing mind--
crossword puzzles, even.

Her Tortoise Shells and Od Maine Coons,
'though sometimes leavin' life too soon
bring joy worth the leavin'.

She speed-reads mysteries oftimes;
prefers those set in British climes
with genteel players

like Christie's Marple and Poirot,
Lord Peter Wimsey, no doubt more
who spring from Sayers.

But nothing brings Nurse J. more joy
than a certain girl and boy--
they play her granny heartstrings.

So, as she makes that turn to sixty,
young Meg and Sean will no doubt fix the
pangs that sometimes age brings.

Harmonic Re-Convergence

Some here today loved Jack or Ronda as they were
before they found each other,
and might perceive this wedding as a completion
of Ronda through Jack, or of him through her.

Overlapping that group, and I among them, are those
who witnessed their mutual discovery—those days
when their faces shone with
"it is,
        it's really happening!";

who shared their astonishment at how perfectly
and how intensely
they fit into each others' lives;

we are the ones, too, who agonized
when diverging needs pulled them apart;
who watched Ronda move forward with her life
while Jack moved forward with his—
 separately, it seemed.

We are the ones who witnessed then
the miracle all of us hope for
and experience all too seldom:
the miracle of re-convergence
as currents, seemingly channeled apart,
rush together again.

Today we celebrate, we celebrate,
each for reasons unique to each
and for reasons common to us all
this miracle of re-convergence.

We gather to celebrate—
and we gather to say to this good couple,
to these two beautiful people,

we gather to say:

go forth in your life together
with our gladness and our love
for who you are
           now.

❦ For Greg-at-41

In observance of your birthday, I find joy
in opening a gift that you bestow to me—
one that's with me always, always ready
to be opened when I pause and recollect it

sitting on a shelf inside the heartspace
where I keep the gifts I cherish most.

It is my sense of you, this gift: the tone
and heft and temper of your life, the gentle
essence I perceive and love and carry
with me always, everywhere. And when,

as now, I take this treasure off its shelf,
unwrap and study it anew, I find
qualities that seem familiar, yet
subtly changed since last I looked this closely.

I see the patience and persistence always
close at hand, a crucial ligature
for your endeavors, firmly backing
the play of intellect as fleet as Hermes.

Next I see: affection for the critters,
woods, and waters; comfort, knowledge, lines
of force that link you with the primal world
and map the journey of your life within it.

Then I glimpse a facet of the gift
I had not noticed until now: how
your journey through the primal world sustains
the most delightful aspects of your essence—

the humor bubbling forth to light your way
through dark and heavy times, for one; and fierce,
unwavering love, for another—qualities
nourished and conditioned by your life in nature.

I notice too, as you near completion of a project
that has harshly tested all your strengths, the current
coursing through these vibrant gifts that you bestow
becoming ever deeper—deeper than you seem to know.

❦ Grateful Dead

Listening to the Grateful Dead version of
"Goin' Down the Road Feelin' Bad,"
wondering if my dad, who loved country & western,
had heard this he would have understood
the transition of his music to mine.

Grateful Dead, you hung a shimmering
musical tapestry before us,
played and sang a consciousness that
will not be broken.

You, Jerry, a pure voice
from America's beat soul,
whanging on into its farthest
reaches of wild
melodic go-to-hell
trans-rational stark beautiful
here-we-are BEING!

The rest of you: Weir, Hart,
Hunter, Lesh, McKernan,
Kreutzman, bringing
your brilliance, your training,
your love, in service to the awakening
of the world to America's true genius.

Some of us still get it
some of the time;
carry the music with us and
tremble with its joy. And some

fold into their own music
your spirit, your licks.
Hence, whether picked off
by chemical bullets or joyfully
surviving and playing,
you, The Dead, live on.

Cass, 39

From a seven-month premie
to a triple-thirteen
full-grown, outright,
forthright, day-and-night,
help-you-out anyway he can
man;
that's what we're lookin' at
today, brothers and sisters—
lookin' at Cass.

And if you tilt your head a bit,
behind him you will glimpse some stretches
of the road he got here by—
from its rocky start, bumped out of the womb
by a car crash seven weeks shy of full-term,
half-alive in a Kaiser incubator,
then a crib at home when it seemed his
body would survive. But only when the time arrived
for his scheduled day of birth did his soul
drop in, so full vitality could begin
to carry that frail frame forward
to its future—to its now.

And what about the road between
that wavering start and robust now?
Here's the short account: vitality infused a complex soul
that absorbed along the road yet more vitality,
which in turn enabled growing complexity—a looping
leaping dance upon the road that led him to this day.

Among us kindred souls allowed by grace to groove with him
along his path, Cass still tosses, as he always has,
sparkle-packets of love and joy and play.

Among us kindred souls he dances yet. His road
continues to unfold and we behold him moving on it,
a mature man of well-earned grace and power,
of wisdom still unfurling, of love whose scope and temper
he continues to uncover.

Hand to hand and heart to heart
we join our several roads with his
to share our energies and love with him
as long as grace permits.

The Snow Beneath Cassiopeia
(for Priscilla Dawson)

She weighed the options: stay alone
in her cold, dark house with limited food
and no way to prepare it,
for no telling how long;
or
suit up and make the mile-long trek
to the warm, generator-powered inn
down by the interstate.

That would be tricky, she thought, with the burden
of all these years and one uncertain knee,
along lightless snowpacked streets,
trees toppling everywhere
(she had heard one snap earlier—
a startling crack in the eerie silence—
and crash nearby).   Still, the notion
of being on the move had more appeal
than eating crackers by candlelight
by herself, waiting
for a tree to fall on her roof.
She packed a kit, dressed in layers,
carried a ski pole for balance.

She got as far as the foot of her driveway, where
a snowplow had left a berm much higher than her head.
Climb it one step at a time, she thought, just the way
Edmund
Hillary
did it.

No good.

In slow motion
she fell back. Deep snow
eased the impact.
Struggling was futile, she found;
the snowy cushion gave no purchase
for turning or lifting her body,
but held her striving limbs confined
until she was exhausted. Calling out
brought no help. She lay still.

I will not die here, she thought, watching
the flakes float gently down.

Time passed.

The snowflakes became raindrops
bathing her face, soaking through her clothes,
then becoming snowflakes again.

More time passed.

The clouds parted for a while, and she watched
Cassiopeia drift leisurely toward the horizon.
She felt deep peace rise up within her.
Her own horizon was sleep, and toward it
she drifted.

When she awoke there was light enough
for her to see her watch and know
she had lain in snow for a long winter's night.
Her right hand, numb and sluggish,
still knew its function well enough to raise
the ski pole toward the clouds and wave it slowly.

I knew I would not die here, she thought, as a
neighbor came to solve the mystery
of a ski pole waving slowly back and forth
above the deepening snow.

VII

"...the happy highways where I went and cannot come again."

—A. E. Housman

Adolescent Nights

Those early years in Los Alamos—
latency and adolescence—tuned in
to the night forces
upturned black and shiny like the horn
of a rare rhinoceros—

the forces of night tingling in my body,
evoking a scent weighty and tinged with musk;
magical night, cloaking and coaxing,
alive with stars,
promising paradise, not out there, right here,
in the moving dark!

But somehow
never quite now.

Growing up on the Pajarito Plateau, I gazed
east toward the Sangre de Cristo Range
across the valley of the Rio Grande
almost daily, through all weathers:

under winter sky, pale blue and streaked with cirrus clouds
or dark, swirling with snow;
I studied the landmarks on the slopes of the Sangres—
Superman "S", Horse Head, Thunderbird—as they whitened;

come spring I yearned for the snow and slush to fade,
for the cutting wind to die, for the juniper pollen
to abandon its annual assault on my eyes and nose,
for the first pale green of aspens there across the valley;

in glorious summer I marveled at the thunderstorms—
the crack and roll and flashing march of lightning
over old Spanish Colonial villages—at how suddenly
the storms would give way to brilliant sunlight and turquoise sky;

through the magic of autumn, of moisture receding and light peaking,
the sky so deeply blue it would stun me, the oak and aspen
reds and yellows so luminous they would pierce my heart,
the joy fleeting and bittersweet.

As autumn's magic fled too quickly, so did the magic of my childhood,
of my youth, of all the weathers my life has relished up to this one,
which has no name that I have heard. Old age it is not, but some
threshold season of uncertain duration with its own joy, fascination,
magic.

Today in Northern New Mexico the Rio Grande is sucked nearly dry,
the aquifer draining fast, the foothills of the Sangres barren with drought
and clotted with trophy homes, new four-lanes across the valley choked
with SUVs belching fumes that obscure the enchanting light
their drivers have paid so much money to enjoy.

Memories of the Mesa

Polar evening light splashes
against clouds remaining
from afternoon monsoon rain, drenches
the tawny velvet top of Black Mesa, and shines
on its rain-slick rim.

To the east, a rainbow emerges
from misty turbulence darkening
over the peaks of the Sangre de Cristo.
A band of corrugated quicksilver,
the Rio Grande slides
intimately around the base of the mesa
and through the still-moist bosque.

Earth and rock seem to swell
upward toward the fleeting light.
Darkening trees lean in
toward the sinuous river as if seeking
its translucence. My sympathetic flesh and bones,
rock and clay of my body,
lean in with the trees.

From the turbulent mists
of my mind emerges, like a rainbow,
a knowing: no matter where the sight
is focused, out or in,
earth persists in seeking light
and yang is unreflected without yin.

With Us Now

That day in the mountains
meandering along the Valle Grande rim
your gold-flecked shoulder
moving with mine in the free-falling sunlight

we had to sprint for cover beneath a blue spruce
as a late summer shower rolled over us
eastward toward the badlands

I thought:

the energy that has seen us through so far
is with us now.

Raven Etiquette

I crept silently—or so I thought—to the edge
of a basalt-rimmed canyon to investigate
the odd sounds coming from somewhere below,
leaned
ever - so - slowly
to peer over the rim,

saw a pair of ravens perched
on a ledge ten feet below, facing out, discussing,
it seemed to me, something of great interest.
As my head cleared the rim (nobody
was ever quieter than I was, looking over that rim),
they stopped their conversation.

One glanced up at me over its shiny black shoulder,
evidently un-alarmed, for neither one flew from the ledge.
     They just shut up.

Sorry to intrude,
I murmured as I backed away. (It's a good practice,
I decided right then,
always to be polite to ravens.)

Someplace I Belong

Up late
by myself in a rented house, I listen:
December wind moans
and shakes the windows.

Warmed by the fire, dreamy with wine,
I watch the seven Yeiis ,
kilted and feather-draped Navajo demigods
aligned across a soft and earthy rug,
appear to sway in unison.

Their movement brings a memory of drumbeats,
lulls me into a vision
of distant prairies—
        grama grass and sagebrush
         on gypsum loam
laced by ribrock matrix—home
to my ancestors and, earlier,
to antelope and buffalo.

For too long I have moved
along pitted asphalt and cracked concrete,
so far away
from rolling plains and playas and mesquite.

When sweet spring rains come
pooling oily rainbows on the cluttered street
and raising stinks of creosote and chemical leaks
in chain-link storage yards,

I still yearn for a trace
of damp prairie fragrance
and a flickering glimpse of antelope.

A Morning in the Sun

Returning home from a morning in the sun,
I felt that gulpy, heart-leaning-over-a-chasm
deep-body pang that often rushes through me when
I have just left, for an unknown time,
someone I love.

We had climbed the grassy hill
above Bon Tempe lake and sat,
hypnotized by glistening water,
talking of our dreams.
The Sleeping Princess, towering beyond,
had cast her benevolent spell
over us and the woods behind,
infusing our voices, the bird songs, the cicadas' hum,
with languid summer magic.

Afterwards, Susan moved on
and I made my way home.

I am happy here
but Susan's presence is only a whisper.
My heart leans forward to hear,
and sags
as the whisper fades away.

Cathedral at Sand Flat

Alone on a Thursday afternoon, late September, I drive up the Memorial Highway, park in our usual place by the road in to Sand Flat. I sit in the car for a few minutes, thinking about your phone call, unsettled by your being ill so far from home. Three o'clock, utterly quiet and still, cloudless sky.

Leaving the car, I walk up the road a quarter-mile to the path we found that climbs to Bunny Flat, go along that for a way, then veer left off the path through old growth Red Fir that graces this part of Mt. Shasta like a living cathedral.

With the sun at my back I zig-zag as spirit wills, always more-or-less toward the peaks glimpsed occasionally through the trees, ascending gradually, going from grove to meadow to grove, casually looking for a likely place to sit and transmit.

I come to what looks like an overgrown roadbed—probably an old skid track—one of the signs of logging here long ago. The second-growth trees are widely spaced, opening up views of Shasta to the east and Mt. Eddie to the west. Looking south, I see an intriguing boulder eighty yards away, right beside the roadbed. I amble over there and examine the hunk of granite. It's about two-and-a-half feet high, three feet across, almost perfectly flat and level on top as if it had been sheared off—but I see no matching pieces nearby. The rock seems perfect for sitting.

I look at the terrain around me. Sloping slightly upward toward Casaval Ridge to the east, it is decorated with scattered groves of Red Fir, all ages. Shasta towers northeast of me. I take out my compass and line up the SSW direction, sit facing that way, the peaks at my back. Behind and far beyond them lie the North Pole, Stockholm, and you.

I meditate for a while in the way I learned from Lawrence LeShan more than thirty years ago. Except for a few birdcalls, the forest abides in utter silence. The pungent odor of coyote mint permeates the air; I use it like a candle to keep my attention focused.

Then I turn to the opposite direction, which puts me facing the hogback between Thumb Rock and Shastarama, and, visualizing you directly before me over the curve of the earth, in Stockholm—after midnight there by now, your brainwaves in delta—subside into the oneness of your self-my self. I lose any sense of time passing, yet when I look around, the sun has drifted discernibly toward the horizon.

    As I stand up, I look at the flat surface of the boulder and succumb to the impulse to leave a symbol on it. Looking around, I find a small hunk of red tufa nearby, which serves as chalk to draw a Zia sun-symbol. Using the compass to line it up, taking my time, I render a very passable circle and rays--three in each cardinal direction, the middle of each three longer than the other two. The rays on the north happen to point directly toward the Heart, below and to the right of Shasta summit.

    Realizing the sketch will disappear with the next rain, I unsheath my Leatherman and use its awl to scratch over the design so that some trace, however slight, will remain. I think of the Anasazi cave-paintings and petroglyphs I've seen on the Pajarito Plateau in northern New Mexico—same impulse 800 years ago.

    Ambling back toward the car, following no path, I come upon two other medicine wheels in the forest a quarter-mile apart, laid out on the ground with rocks.

    Five o'clock sun shafts slanting in low throw light helter-skelter through the cathedral. I hear my footstep crunches as moving chants, and pause frequently to gather the forest hush.

    I reach the car just as the sun slides behind a nearby ridge. Full of the forest, I drive through the forest, downward, toward home.

June 17, Rain

Ranging in reverie with the black and turquoise
forces of a rainy night, this way,
that way, chucked around,
train whistle, fog horn, then
a leafier variation settles in: I sense
a deep being
in a cloud of chlorophyll—
green quivering within fibrous boundaries—
memory drifts to the 19 year-old college boy walking
the streets of New Orleans, mid-50s:
Calhoun up to South Claiborne and the Toddle House Diner;
St. Charles over to Carrolton, or the other direction—
all the way to Canal Street one Sunday morning—
wandering on Freret, Napoleon, through the neighborhoods
night and day. All over the Quarter, all hours,
usually alone, protected only
by innocence and wonder.

I sometimes blunder past the hub,
ignoring chances for retraction.
Indiscretions pile up and stretch
the boundaries of acceptability.
My allies have a tough time
keeping me from great harm,
but they almost always succeed.

Midnight—still raining.
Still a sense of black and turquoise,
and still a quivering green.

Seven Scandinavian Women

Since our arrival yesterday on Nagu Island
a strong north wind has pushed
intermittent rain across
the Finnish Archipelago.

Now at twilight, head slightly bowed,
I walk directly into the wind,
dodging puddles on a dirt road
and once—recapturing
the agility of my youth—shift

sharply to the left
        aikido-like
to avoid getting splashed
by a fast-moving farm truck.

Turning right onto a narrow lane
I trudge up a steep slope through
birch and conifer forest toward
a rustic, two-story wooden building

where I will dine with seven
Scandinavian women and
my California-born wife.

Large African tapestries
line the walls of a spacious dining room where
the women, seated at two tables,
have begun their salad course

when I walk in. The conversation,
at once lively and serene,
pauses as I take a seat
next to Marina, a "Swedish-speaking Finn,"

who is hosting us for eleven days.

Before me on the table sit
a salad plate, already served,
a small glass that Marina
promptly fills with wine,
and a larger glass

that soon holds water with lime.
Alert glances greet me, and smiles
that hint of underlying zest—
the tingly taste of lime in water.

One man among eight poised
and powerful women, I remember
to breathe and open to their power,
to drink it in like wine, to let it

tingle through me
as lime through water.

"When we have shuffled off this mortal coil"

—William Shakespeare

The Northshore Trail

We walk up the northshore trail
through light rain, conversation
relaxed and wide ranging
from visionary dreams through
challenges of her work.

First time on this trail in rain
we agree. Been here through snow some,
many times in fair weather.

Contemplating the change in seasons
I enter a wrenching, lucid awareness of time
passing quickly, and of
the late season my life has entered.

With the awareness, an image: A blue heron
dying on the far shore of the lake,
wings moving slowly
in remembered flight;
overnight, the water rises to submerge
       flowers
and half of one pulsing wing.

Kinder Options, Please

Alerted by the distant roar of surf
breaking on a rocky beach,
I might as well accept, it seems,
the likelihood it could be my turn
to be a leaky skiff adrift on choppy seas.

                  The trans-substantiation of a soul—
does it involve subsiding into cold
and murky waters like those
that surge around the Farallones,
where Great White sharks in silent hosts
assemble, flirt, and breed before adjourning
to bother seals and surfers up and down the coast?
Could my soul's new casing then be torpedo-shaped,
tough-skinned, and armed with teeth out to here—
doomed to move incessantly, provoking fear?

                  Or would my soul float up instead
to take on feathers and a beak and feed
on garbage jettisoned by ships en route
from Hong Kong to the Golden Gate?

                  I suppose my soul might billow out—
become the fog that cloaks those ships
and quietly engulfs the coastal hills
to keep the redwoods watered
through the rainless summers
until they're rendered into logs.

But if I could find a current that might bear
this slowly sinking vessel into quiet harbor,
I would gladly seek to join with it—
not at all too proud to ask
for kinder options, please.

Wings

Wings beating hard, his life
lifted through five decades,
then six, then seven,
up through currents that

swung one way, then another, defying
prediction and control
but somehow always keeping him aloft.
Through those decades, at the center

and edges of his vision he saw
companions fall away,
willed his life to loop around,
so he could try to ease their fall;

then, when those beloved ones
sank one by one from sight,
his life swung back, continued climbing,
tacking toward the unknown distance.

Came a time
when his life could
still its wings, and soar,
could circle over all
the scraps his shadow had traversed
and tagged as if they would
one day be useful,

could soar over the papers, books,
sights, sounds, sensations;
doings, thrills, regrets—
all the attributed meanings
he had believed would count
and be preserved, would somehow

amount to something—and
could deem most of them worthwhile.
Eventually the feathers began falling
from those once-sturdy wings
and he began looking around
for who might still be there,
who would care, to ease
his own certain
descent.

Jim Brown is a semi-retired mind-body specialist and eternal information sponge living in Mt. Shasta, California with his original wife, Molly Brown. He has a doctorate in the psychology of consciousness, and with such a background knows very well the addictive potential of activity that serves both to soothe and stimulate. Still, he goes on writing poems and such, which for him is an activity that does exactly that.

www.ingramcontent.com/pod-product-compliance
Lightning Source LLC
Chambersburg PA
CBHW031255290426
44109CB00012B/586